Horse Training

Complete Owners Guide to Horse Training

By

SaddleUP

Horse Training

Are You Ready to Saddle Up?

Easy Training * Fast Results

Horse Owner's Horse Book

Saddle Up Horse Training Books

By

Kelly O. Callahan

The Author

Kelly O. Callahan & Cedar

About the Author

I am 58-years-young and have owned horses for the last 10-years. I have been caring for horses and training them 24/365 those 10 years. My brother owned a pony when I was 5 years old. That was the first and only time I was kicked by a horse. During my lifetime, I gravitated towards horses and would ride every chance I had. I hope you enjoy training your Horse!

Dedication

This book is dedicated to my Sherry longtime life partner over twenty-years. Sherry is my inspiration and helped me to grow into a confident and courageous new author.

I'm Ready, Thank You.

Let's Saddle Up!

Table of Contents

Introduction

Hi there. Did you just get a new Horse? There are over 9 million horses in the United States. Less than 1 million are registered horses. That means most horses purchased in the United States are from undocumented lineage and the actual breed is not always known. These intelligent and beautiful creatures may be the best friend you have ever had. If you have not already had dressage or riding lessons, then do that now. Your safety must always come first. Horses can be extremely dangerous. If you have not yet purchased your Horse, then consider having a Vet check before you commit to a purchase. Whether a 2-year old or 10-20-year-old horse, you just got (or will get) a new best friend who will warm and enrich your life for up to a 35-year life span. You made a great choice by letting a Horse into your life.

Your new Horse will never betray your secrets or leave you for someone else. He will stay by your side, loving you for a lifetime to come, be a great addition to your family, and he'll provide all your loved ones with years of joy. Your Horse can perform work for you, and alert you to danger. You will get hours of amusement, and maybe even some hilariously cute, and fun filled viral Internet videos with your best friend. The benefits of Horse ownership are too many to be counted.

Your relationship with your Horse must be a positive one. No one wants a wild Horse who cannot be controlled, or worse, an aggressive and mean Horse who is no fun to be around. Establishing a good relationship with your Horse from the minute you bring him home will ensure that the years to come are good years. Starting a good relationship with your Horse involves plenty of training. Don't let this overwhelm you. You will love every minute. *You Got This!*

If you start training *your Horse* right away and use the methods outlined in this book, you will have no problem raising a nice and responsive Horse who respects you and will do what you want, when you want, on your command. Horses are naturally loyal and loving creatures who want to please their best friend and master - *you.* You must teach him how to please. Teach him that your word is law and that he needs to mind you. In this guide, you will learn everything you need to know about training your Horse. You will learn how to check him properly to end problem behaviors before they would get out of hand. You will also learn how to have your Horse obey basic commands and even perform great under the saddle.

This book covers everything from long lead training, round pen training and hand cues, and verbal commands. Your relationship with your Horse is not just about training. It is mostly about bonding with you. You want to bond with your Horse in the right way. In the following chapters, you will learn how to become the alpha, so that your Horse minds you. At the same time, you will learn how to be able to love him and have fun with him. Your Horse craves your commanding alpha presence and voice. But being alpha does not mean that you can't have loads of fun with your Horse. It also does not mean that you must act or be mean or aggressive. Firmness is what you are going for, not meanness.

You also need to know how to care for your Horse. Your new Horse needs proper nutrition, grooming and veterinarian care to stay healthy. You can prevent or mitigate health problems down the road by feeding your Horse properly, having on-site Vet checks every year for check-ups, getting his shots and wormers on time, exercising him mentally, physically, and grooming him correctly. Everything you need to know about caring for Horse is covered in Chapter 2.

When you get your Horse, like most of we humans, you probably want a best friend. This best friendship is only possible if you act now and teach your Horse to respect and obey you. It is also crucial that you form a friendship with your Horse where he looks up to you as his master but also trusts you and wants to be around you. Being gentle but firm with your Horse from *day one* is paramount to forming that lasting and trusting loyalty that will never die.

Therefore, if you are ready to start turning your new Horse into a good boy (or girl) he/she wants to be now, read on. This Horse training book will help you form a best friendship with a loving, loyal Horse who craves your attention and comes at your command. You will complete this guide knowing how to care for your friend, how to stop bad behavior and how to teach and reward good behavior.

You will also learn other cool stuff, such as breed-specific facts and keys to understanding your Horse's communication since he cannot speak.

Chapter 1

Horse Bio

You got yourself a Horse. That is wonderful, because Horses are eager to train, and loyal. You will love getting to know and train your new best friend. First however, you should learn a few things about the animals to understand how to train your Horse in the ideal way. They will require stimulation, exercise and attention. Horses are recognized as ideal family pets due to their easy-going and affectionate demeanor. Do not let the bad reputation of maybe a hot blood horse scare you if that is what you want.

Horses may be possessive of their space and food but are generally an excellent pet if you are introducing your Horse into a small herd, make sure you take the introduction slowly and don't force any animal to be friend the other. Horses can be tall, slim, athletic, and some are under 15 hands. In fact, they range 14-18 hands depending on the breed of horse that you choose.

The Horse was first domesticated around 4000 BC. It is believed the domesticated horse was widespread around 3000 BC. There are three main categories of horses. Hot blooded horses including Arabians and Thoroughbreds. Warm bloods include

Quarter Horses. Cold bloods are draft horses such as Clydesdales and Belgian Horses.

The Thoroughbred breed was started in England in the 1680s. All modern Thoroughbred Horses are traced back to three Arabian Stallions. Byerley Turk in the 1680s, the Darley Arabian in 1704, and the Godolphin Arabian in 1729. The addition of the Eastern Stallions with the native English Racehorse Mares led to the creation of the General Stud Book in 1791. This became the official registration of horses.

Horse racing continued evolving in England to include longer races up to 4 miles. The first Thoroughbred Horse to come to the American Colonies was Bulle Rock in 1730. Horse racing growth in America is due to the Thoroughbred Horse, but the Thoroughbred horse was used to improve other breeds. The Thoroughbred Horse was the foundation of the Standardbred, the Quarter Horse, and the Morgan breed. The Thoroughbred Horse also were exported to France, Australia, and New Zealand. Later Thoroughbred Horses were exported to South Africa and Argentina.

The value of a Thoroughbred racehorse has increased over the centuries. In 2006, the highest price paid at auction for a 2-year-old colt named The Green Monkey was $16,000,000.00. Ultimately, this horse never won a race (due to injuries) and was retired to stud in 2008. Stud fees for stallions can range from $2500.00 to $500,000.00 per mare in the USA. The highest stud fee recorded was $1,000,000 in the 1980s for the late stallion Northern Dancer.

Horses were often used for racing but are used for many other events. Thoroughbreds excel at show jumping and combined training. Many retired racehorses become great family horses, youth show horses, and dressage horses. The larger horses are often used in dressage competitions and hunter/jumper events. Smaller Horses are used as polo ponies.

The modern Thoroughbred is larger than the horse in 1700ad. Less than 50% of all racehorses ever win a race. Less than 1% ever win a stakes race like the Kentucky Derby. The horses who have never won a race are often entered in to a "Maiden Race", where none of the horses entered has ever won a race. The non-winning horses are known as Maidens. The horses who have retired from racing and are not suitable for breeding often are adopted out for riding horses or other reasons.

History

Flat racing took place in England in 1174 or earlier. After the middle ages horse racing became a royal event and Kings became interested. Then handicapping was devised to equalize the horses in the event. The favored horses were required to carry extra weight to even the playing field. The term "thro-bred" was first used to describe the breed in 1713.

One famous early import was Janus, a Thoroughbred who was the grandson of the Godolphin Arabian. He was foaled in 1746 and was imported to Virginia in 1756. The Godolphin Arabian was one of the three Arab Stallions whose genes are present in all modern Thoroughbred Horses. Approximately 160 other Arabian Stallions were later added to the gene pool.

What to Expect when Training a Horse

Horses are very easy to train. You simply must assert yourself as the alpha. Immediately start disciplining and training your Horse to show him who is in charge. Begin from the moment you bring him home in the horse trailer. He will quickly accept you as the leader and work hard to please you. The process varies and can take from one month to over one year, depending on the Owner and the Horse. The important thing is that you are enjoying every moment and that your focus is to try to make the Horse enjoy it as well.

When you choose your Horse, be sure to find one who is already saddle-broke and is ready to ride. Try to find one who already seems friendly and seems to like you. Over 90% of the Horses purchased in the United States are already trained to this point. Most Horses are saddle-broke when they are around 2 years of age.

Most Horses purchased are 5+ years old and have been ridden under saddle for several years. Please note, this is not a book on how to saddle-break a Horse, it is a book to train your Horse to be your best and most reliable friend. When you purchase your Horse, they know nothing about you. They do not even know that you now own him and have the goal to be his best friend.

Horses typically do not need lots of harsh discipline. When you have a halter on and you are holding the rope, a quick "check" or tug on the lead rope will get his attention if he is acting up in some way. Once you show him that a behavior is undesirable, he will learn not to do it.

You want to socialize your Horse to ensure that he grows up into a well-rounded and normal animal. You also want to keep him active. A common problem that people encounter with Horses is boredom. A bored Horse may develop odd habits such as "cribbing" (chewing on a fence rail), pacing back and forth, or "weaving" back and forth.

If you own and live on the horse property where your Horse lives, then you can make sure he gets as much pasture time as possible. If you "board" your Horse at a local stable you can expect to pay from $200.00 per month for full pasture board, and up to $600.00 per month for full care including a stall, paddock and daily pasture time.

We do not recommend that you keep your Horse in a stall with short turn-out time unless your main objective is a show-horse. Most Horses cannot tolerate that level of captivity. Keep him active with hard exercise and running in his pasture or turnout. Be sure to exercise him while training to ensure that he is more attentive. After you have given your Horse a few days to get acclimated to his new living environment, it is a good time to bring him out of the stall on his rope and halter to begin his training. Begin with some simple commands as you lead him around. "Walk, stand, walk, stand", and once you utter a command, you'll get a kick out of how fast your Horse learns.

Enjoy your Horse!

Chapter 2

Fun Facts about Your Horse

- Horses are naturally loving animals and aim to please their owners.

- Quarter Horses are one of the fasted breeds of horses in races up to ¼ mile

- All Thoroughbred Horses have some Arabian Horse blood in their genes

- Some Thoroughbred Horses have been clocked at 43.97 miles per hour in short distances

- Horses excel at show jumping and combined training

- Many retired racehorses become great family horses, youth show horses, and dressage horses

- The larger horses are often used in dressage competitions and hunter/jumper events

- Smaller Horses are used as polo ponies

- The Horse is most often used today as a racehorse, rodeo competitions, show horse, reining and cutting horse, ranch horse, and all-around family horse

Chapter 3

Socializing Your Horse

How to Condition Your Horse to Get Along with Everyone

Socializing your Horse from an early start is essential. Do you know why? Because a horse who is socialized well is not aggressive to or scared of dogs or people. He knows that dogs and people exist and are not necessarily threats to his safety. A horse that is not socialized, on the other hand, feels as if the world is a threat and reacts in fear. He gets scared and threatened when other dogs or people show up. So as soon as you bring your Horse home, you need to start socializing him. Get him used to having other people and dogs in his life.

Attitude (Yours)

Your attitude is very transparent to your Horse. He can read you like a book. When you are upset with him, he can sense it. He can also sense when you are in a bad mood, and he won't understand that your bad mood has nothing to do with him. Therefore, during the process of socialization, you should always have a good attitude and be assertive. Your Horse will bond better when he gets good vibes from you. Always be patient, gentle, encouraging, and loving.

Show more pride and happiness than anger or frustration. If you do get frustrated, step aside for a minute, take a deep breath, and try a new activity with your Horse, then return once you feel calm, cool and collected. Positivity is going to be your key to success when training your Horse. Don't keep pushing your Horse or getting mad or you will ruin the training experience and overall results for both of you.

A huge part of socializing your Horse is conditioning him to become the type of horse that you want him to be when you are riding him later. The Horse he grows into is largely shaped during the first several months of his training. Therefore, you want to do the most work during this period and focus on your end goal. (The earlier the better is the rule of thumb when training) So have a plan, and stick to it, be consistent, *know* what you expect of him and make it clear. Really get happy and excited when he does what you want and reward him handsomely for desirable behavior.

When you follow these principals, you can be amazed at how great you are at training your new Horse. Another huge part of socializing is forging the special bond that you want to share with your Horse for the rest of his life. You must do this by teaching him that you are the herd-leader. But you also want to teach him that you love him and that you two are best friends. If you take the right approach outlined in this training guide and treat your Horse like a best friend from the beginning, he will become the most loyal and loving friend that you have ever had. Approach socializing with the attitude that you want to be friends with this Horse but be sure to also show that you are the dominant friend and the herd-leader. Be gentle but firm. Provide direction without being mean or aggressive. Firmness is always better than aggression when socializing a Horse.

When and How to Socialize Your Horse

Your Horse already began the socialization process when he is just a few hours old. Until then, he socializes with his mother and maybe a few other horses if available. Of course, you cannot just expect a Horse to learn how to be a good riding horse from his mom. The Horse must be exposed to humans and get used to human contact from a very young age. Simply because this is the most impressionable time of a horse's life and it really shapes your Horse as he matures. Your Horse is a bit older when you invite him in your life, don't worry about your effectiveness in training him. You will just need to spend a bit more time on it. From the minute you get your Horse, you need to start handling him properly as the alpha. Move his body, pet him, and talk with him. Get him used to being handled by humans. Brush him every time you take him out of his stall. He will learn that you mean no harm, this is enjoyable, and that he is safe with his new human herd-leader. Expose your Horse to multiple environments. Take him outside, on rides, go out on a trail where there is plenty of grass, plants, other animals, and a few people, walking, exploring and picnicking. Take him to the beach, a lake, a stream, a pond or your local lake. You get the gist here. Have fun with it, get creative and introduce him to several different landscapes, from natural settings to beaches and trails. Depending on your circumstances, you may need to walk down a gravel road to get to a trail and he may be exposed to a car passing slowly.

Traffic, planes, trains and automobiles maybe sounds your Horse is exposed to. He will become acclimated to all the different environments and sounds he is exposed to. If you are taking your Horse to various environments, you may need to take him in a horse-trailer. This teaches him that's it's okay to be curious rather than afraid of many different and new things. A worldly Horse is a good horse.

When you have friends over, let them meet your Horse so that he gets used to them and learns to like different people. You don't want him to get overly attached to you so that he distrusts other people. Spend a lot of time bonding with your Horse, because it will unite the two of you tightly. It also teaches him what is acceptable and what is not when it comes to interacting with you, and others. It teaches him that you are a good, trustworthy owner who loves him and being with you entails happy, fun times. It's a good idea to find and create lots of mentally stimulating and physical activities to keep him engaged and active. *Note: It's imperative to give your Horse some alone time. This teaches him not to be anxious when you are not available to bond with him. Put him in his paddock or pasture by himself for at least an hour or two a few times a day to let him graze. Let him out to be by himself or with other horses, but not you.*

Don't be afraid to correct your Horse to prevent bad habits early on. If he nips you on the arm, tell him "No" firmly. Tell him "No" when he fidgets while being brushed at the hitching rail. If you teach him early on what is *allowed* and what is not, he will grow into a more obedient horse and you will have less corrective action further down the road.

Stopping any bad behavior and replacing it with a good one will show him that you are the boss and he needs to mind you. Believe it or not, he craves this from you. Let him know which behaviors are acceptable and which are not, starting right away. Be firm, not cruel.

Avoid physical punishment and yelling, as these actions can traumatize your Horse for a lifetime. You don't wish him to be afraid of you, but to respect you with pride in his heart. All it takes is a firm 'No' and redirection to another activity to change a behavior while disciplining your Horse. Now, it's time to start lightly training your Horse. Of course, we cover that in depth through-out this horse training book.

Also introduce him to his Stall and Paddock and show him that the stall is a safe place where he can go for peace and quiet and shelter from the weather. Never use the paddock as punishment or you will make him grow up to hate the paddock and avoid it at all costs. You will soon learn that your Horse loves his paddock and associates it with safety, grains, vitamins, hay and fresh water.

You will need to schedule a farm call from your trusted Veterinarian to ensure your Horse is up to date on worming, and vaccinations, and in good health. Listen to all recommendations including feeding, training, and exercise and if there are any health concerns.

Watch your Horses hooves and when they get long, and then schedule a hoof trimming with your trusted Farrier. Listen to all recommendations including if your Horse has strong hooves or would do better with shoes. Some recommendations you will choose to follow.

Attitude (Yours)

After your Horse is acclimated to his paddock, you need to begin serious training. Meaning, at this time, you can successfully teach him things in the round pen or on a long lead rope. You will learn all about this in our upcoming chapters. Be sure to walk with him to get him conditioned to the world around him. Expose him to a wide variety of people, horses and places to get him over any fears and show him to accept the world as it is. Socializing lasts for the Horse's entire life. You can't lock him in the paddock and never expose him to other people and expect him to be normal around them when he encounters them again. Socializing and training your Horse, is a lifelong journey. Small steps every day will go a long way.

Fear Imprinting and Overcoming

Keep in mind that horses go through fear imprinting phases. During these phases, your horse can develop phobias. Any negative stimuli can leave a lasting impression on your horse, creating a fear that endures for the rest of his life.

For example, your horse might become afraid of all men if a man is abusive toward him during this phase. Or he might become afraid of kids if a child is always pulling on his tail.

To avoid creating fear in your horse, try to avoid exposing him to frightening things, like loud noises such as fireworks on the 4th of July, yelling in anger, or avoidable pain inflicting actions. Don't discipline him over zealously at any time of his life, instead be gentle. Expose him to things like traffic, loud music, and other normal environmental stimuli by taking him for regular walks around the stables, in order to condition him to drop the fearful attitude and show him that most stimulus is harmless. The more you expose him to the real world around him, the less afraid he will be.

Of course, some horses develop weird phobias. My horse was afraid of leaving the stables by himself and with no other horses with him. I gradually took him further and further each day. Each day I would make him go a bit further and stand for 5 minutes before returning. I spoke to him each time repeating over and over, "Good boy, good boy, good boy." After about 5 minutes we were out far enough he could no longer see the other horses. He did not seem to have any more anxiety about it, so we continued out for a one-hour trail ride. He was never scared of leaving by himself again. It took a whole bag of treats to get over that one *(for both of us)*. On the plus side, we did get plenty of exercise, so there's that.

For instance, your horse might become afraid of walking over a tarp on the grass. I am not sure if he thought he would fall through or slip or trip. Whatever the reason, he did not want to walk on the tarp. This was solved by showing him another horse being led over the tarp and nothing bad happened to the horse. His ears perked straight up, and he looked surprised in his eyes. After that he followed the other horse over the tarp and was never scared about it again. Always be sure to tell him, "good boy" over and over when he overcomes a fear. Let him realize that the things he is afraid of really won't hurt him. Help him develop positive associations instead of negative ones.

If your horse has a bad experience with a person, another horse, or any other animal, he may become timid. But this fear does not have to be permanent if you take care to correct it and recondition him.

It's a good idea to expose him to nice and friendly, happy people, horses and other animals to show him that not everyone is the *Unabomber*. For example, if there is a person visiting the stables that yelled at your Horse you will want to avoid that person for obvious reasons. Expose him to other more gentle and quiet people to help overcome his fear of people. Overcoming fear is a crucial part of socializing your Horse.

You may also want to expose him to different sides of yourself. You can wear a hat; shave your beard if you are an adult male and *have-said-beard*. If you want to that is, besides, (I heard it grows back thicker). You can wear sunglasses, a dress or shorts, instead of slacks or jeans.

You can change your hair style, use a different smelling aftershave, or shampoo too. He will notice these changes. If you continue to talk to him and let him know that everything is OK when you appear different, he will learn to accept that sometimes your appearance or scent changes. Then he won't be so nervous about change.

Read on to find out how to take care of your new best friend.

Chapter 4

Taking Care of Your Horse

Essential Care for Your New Horse

Learning how to care for your Horse starting before you bring your horse home really helps you to mitigate future health problems that he may have. Feeding, grooming, and exercising your Horse properly is essential for each phase of his life. You want to have a vet check before bringing him home. Oh, and be warned at the first visit, chances are he'll resist it or appear fearful. The vet will quickly make friends with him and establish trust for future visits. Keeping him mentally and physically active throughout his life, will help minimize problem behaviors.

Feeding

Equine nutrition is incredibly important for your horse's wellbeing. His nutritional needs will depend on his age, activity level, and breed. Be sure to pick the proper food for his wellbeing. Here is some advice on how to feed your horse, and what types of food you should choose.

Dry Fodder

When picking dry fodder, ensure that the first consideration is past feedings by the previous owner. Many horse owners prefer Alfalfa over grass hay. Alfalfa is a legume and has more protein than grass hay. Some Horses get "jacked up" if they get that much protein. Pay attention if it appears your horse is more energetic or exhibits behavior problems. If you notice this behavior, try grass hay such as Orchard Grass or Timothy Hay for a week and see if the behavior does not occur. If you find that your horse gets jacked up on Alfalfa, you will want to switch to a grass hay diet.

Supplemental Vitamins, Feed or Grain

Select a horse food that offers a rich selection of vitamins and minerals. There are supplements specifically formulated for Young horses, seniors, obese horses, and active horses alike. I like to use a vitamin supplement feed called Super Supplement LMF – G. The G stands for grass hay. Another variety is needed if you are feeding your horse Alfalfa. My Horses get ½ pound of LMF-G every morning and every evening. They also receive 1 pound of COB (a mixture of corn, oats, and barley) twice daily. My oldest senior horse has recently lost some weight, so she gets an extra ½ pound of rice bran twice daily to help her regain her weight.

In the dry seasons the horses are let out into the pasture after the morning feeding for the day. They can graze on the grass most of the day. They can consume approximately one pound of grass per hour. If your horses are out for 10 hours grazing, then you want to make sure each horse is given additional hay overnight. Most Horses, who are 15-hands at the shoulder and highest point of the body, are approximately 1000 pounds. This size horse should have a mixture of pasture and hay to equal 20 pounds daily. On days when it is estimated the horse grazed 10 pounds of grass, then you should give him an additional 10 pounds of hay in the evening for overnight.

Some days you will decide not to let your horse out of the paddock for weather related reasons. On those days you will need to give each horse approximately 20 pounds of hay in the stall. During the early Spring the grass has very high sugar content. Most horses should be limited to a short time in the pasture during the new growth season of the spring. Some years and localities have a second new growth season in the fall. Every part of the country is different so pay attention to your area.

The reason for this limitation of lush, fast growing grass is that your horse can get too much of the sugar content and "founder." A horse that founders can quickly develop laminitis. Laminitis can cripple your horse and can end his life. It is much safer to limit the amount of pasture time to avoid illness during these times of new grass growth.

Wet Food

A wet horse food diet can be useful for a Horse who suffer from old age and lack of teeth. A horse can be given soaked hay pellets to replace the hay if they can no longer chew it. The soaked pellets can be eaten by the horse even with no teeth for years to extend the life of your horse. Generally, after approximately 25 years of age your horse may start losing teeth. It may be about 5 or more years before they must switch to a wet food diet.

Fresh Food Diet

A fresh food diet can be great for your Horse since it more closely mimics what he would eat on his own in the wild. However, you must take care to avoid founder if he is on a strictly pasture diet. Many horses can live without vitamins, grain and supplemental hay. Many horses can live in a pasture 24/7 and never develop laminitis. If your horse is a pasture horse, it is imperative that they have a shelter they can go to, to avoid the heat or wet weather. If your horse is living as a pasture horse, then they need 24/7 access to FRESH, and clean water. An automatic watering system would be recommended.

How Much to Feed your Horse

How much you feed your Horse depends on his stamina, age, activity level, and size. You can gauge it if you should feed your horse more based on whether you can feel his ribs. If his ribs don't stick out, you know that you are feeding enough. If his ribs become covered in fat, you need to cut back on feed. Here is a general guideline for feeding hay or grass: 2% of the horse's body weight each day. This is based on the total amount of estimated pasture grass and/or evening hay.

Remember that this is just a rough guideline that you can adjust as needed. But keep in mind that the average Horse is about 1000 pounds when fully grown, so you would want to feed him roughly twenty pounds of grass and/or hay daily.

When to Feed your Horse

Horses need to eat 24/7 in order to eat at least 20 pounds of Hay each day. I have seen show horses be kept in a stall up to 23-hours per day. I have seen them kept under blankets and heat lamps in the stall in the wintertime. They do this so that the horse will not grow a winter coat. A winter coat is not appealing in the show horse arena. We are assuming that if you have a show horse, you would not likely purchase this book but a more show horse specific training manual.

Most people do not do pasture horse boarding with no daily feeding required. Most Horses will be fed twice daily, morning and evening. After the morning feeding, you will let your horse graze in the pasture for most of the day. After a few days, your Horse will realize that the evening feed means vitamins and some grain. Your Horse will look forward to you calling him into his paddock to get his desired feed. They love vitamins and grain. It is like a treat or a reward. They will quickly learn to come to you calling his name or a shrill sharp whistle. Stand in a safe place when you call him in because he may run straight at you in a full run gallop. It is unlikely your Horse will run you over, but it is safer to stand near a fence post or something that you know he won't run into for your own protection. After a while, you will trust your Horse enough that he will never run you down or touch you while running into their paddock.

If you feed your Horse twice daily, it gives the opportunity for additional training, bonding, and time together. Your Horse will associate you with their feeding of their favorite food (Grain and Vitamins). If you feed your Horse (personally) twice daily, you will go up a notch and will more likely become his favorite human as the result. This dynamic will likely occur sooner if you are the one feeding him.

One big part of horse ownership is establishing that you are the alpha leader in the herd. We cover Alpha Status in our last chapter, for now, what this means is you get to eat first. It may seem trivial, but it's a big contributor to establishing your alpha. Your Horse must wait patiently until it is his turn to eat. Doing this establishes your dominance and teaches your Horse that he does not rule the roost. He may already be waiting in his paddock at feeding time even before you call him in. This will not happen every time, during the high growth season of the grass. During that time, he may prefer the sweet new grass growths over his grain. You may need to go out to your Horse and put a halter on him and lead him to the paddock the first few times to teach him. If he has a pasture mate who comes in right away, it is likely your Horse will follow the first few times.

Switching Foods

At some point it may become apparent a need to switch grain or hay for various reasons. To switch food brands, try this switching schedule:

- Day 1-2 Mix ¼ new with ¾ old foods

- Day 2-4 Mix ½ new with ½ old

- Day 5-6 Mix ¾ new with ¼ old

- Day 7 100% of the new food

When switching your Horse for instance from Alfalfa to Orchard Grass Hay, you should start gradually as noted above. You may notice that your hot blood Horse is getting jacked up on the Alfalfa (due to the higher level of protein) and it is a good idea to try him on Orchard Grass. You will likely notice an improvement in his behavior. If you have a mare horse, you may decide to try some "Mare Magic" (meant to stabilize her mood from her cycles). You will likely notice an improvement in her behavior. Mare Magic can also help a Geldings mood. You may notice your horse is getting too

27

much fat on his ribs and decide to reduce his feed. You may notice you can feel and/or see your horse's ribs and decide to add some rice bran to his diet to bring his weight back up. It is common to change or adjust your Horses feed to maintain optimal health. If you are unsure at any time, it is recommended that you contact your Vet for additional advice.

Healthy Treats and Snacks

Here are some healthy human foods you can offer your Horse in his diet or as treats:

- Oat and molasses treats
- Apples and oat treats
- Apples
- Pears
- Various horses treat from your feed store
- Squash or pumpkin
- Carrots

Exercising Your Horse

Exercise is essential to your Horse's health. Just like people, Horses need exercise to stay healthy. A sedentary Horse is prone to obesity, muscle problems, joint problems, and heart problems as he gets older. On top of that, a lack of exercise can create a bored Horse, which in turn can create an unruly Horse. You want to keep your Horse occupied with plenty of activity, free activity outside in his paddock and with exercise.

Horses require anywhere from thirty minutes to two hours of physical activity a day. Horses need at least two hours of activity and pasture time. You can provide some of this activity just by letting him run around in his pasture. Some of this activity you need to be proactive about. Go into his paddock after he eats his grain in the morning, put his halter on with his lead rope and tie him (with some slack) onto the hitching rail.

Get out his brushes and brush his whole body completely. Brush his tail and mane getting out all the tangles. If you brush your Horse's mane and tail daily, you will not find many tangles the second and third days. If you intend to ride your Horse as part of his exercise for the day, then get his blanket and saddle on after brushing.

It is important to brush your Horse well every time before you put the saddle on. Be sure any burrs, foxtails, and debris are removed from brushing. If you saddle your horse with a burr between his skin and his saddle, you will not have a happy Horse. If this is your first horse and you have never had a lesson, we recommend lessons before you ride your Horse. You can also be taught how to saddle and bridle your Horse. After tightening his cinch of his saddle then you can put on his bridle. Secure his reins to the saddle horn (if western saddle) or around the base of his neck near the saddle (if an English saddle). Attach his long lead rope and lead him to a round pen if you have one or a central space of an empty pasture.

We will discuss specific exercise training later, but essentially you can exercise your Horse with him doing walk, trot, canter in circles around you to warm up his muscles. A general rule of thumb, 10 circles walk to the left, 10 trots, and 10 canters. Then switch directions to the right and repeat, walk, trot, canter to the right. This will warm him sufficiently before riding. It will also help to expend some of his pent-up energy so that he behaves better when riding after.

Now you are ready to ride. You may choose to use a mounting block to reduce lifting your leg high enough for your stirrups. However, it is important that you can mount both ways. Start him out gradually. Ride him 10-15 minutes the first time. The next day 15-20, then 20-25, then keep the pattern until you get up to 1 hour per day. If you are riding in an indoor arena, there should be no issues. If you are leaving the stables to ride on a trail, you may find that your Horse feels scared leaving the stable.

You may have to do some shorter trips when leaving the stables at first. If you have started riding within one week of bringing your Horse to the stables, you are less likely to have problems. If you wait longer than one week, you may notice more fear in your Horse due to a condition referred to as "barn sour." This simply means that your Horse is scared to leave his safe stables for the big scary rest of the world or wilderness.

Horses are prey animals. They are naturally scared of bears or Cougars eating them or if they see a deer or elk, who knows what they are going to do? Be prepared if you run into some strange creature on the trail it is highly likely your horse will react. This can be dangerous to you. Your Horse may try to throw you off his back or jump so far and so fast that you simply fall off. I am not trying to scare you only prepare you. Some Horses will simply freeze and assess the situation. That is the most desired reaction.

If your Horse freezes and assesses the situation, then calmly turn him away from the danger and proceed in that direction at a walk. Do not let him run or even trot away from a predator. The running will often inspire the bear or cougar to automatically chase it. Do not run or let your horse trot. Others will take off at a run in the opposite direction and you may have difficulty controlling him. You may need to jump off or simply hang on and ride it out for a few hundred yards or so.

There are many things you may need to face with your Horse while you are creating a relationship with him. You must be prepared in advance. He may be the love of your life. If you are aware of the dangers and prepare in advance. We recommend that you wear a safety Helmut when riding. We recommend whenever possible to have second rider with you if you are going out on a trail. This physical activity has the added benefit of getting you out and moving too. *Just, saying.*

Grooming:

Brushing

You should brush your Horse's coat at least four times a week and clean his hooves each time. Daily brushing is ideal when a Horse is shedding in the Spring. He will need to shed his entire winter coat before the warm summer comes.

I can assure you it's mutually therapeutic before a long day begins.

This is one of the most therapeutic and bonding experiences you will have with your Horse. He will love to get brushed as much as you like to brush him. Talk to him while you are brushing him. Use his name often while speaking to him. Say, "good boy" every time he is standing properly. If he begins to try to move around or away from you, give the command, "Stand." When he stands still, say "Good Boy", and repeat good boy over and over while he is standing still. Some Horses may try to kick or bite you when they are new. DO NOT LET EITHER HAPPEN EVER! It is your responsibility to keep yourself safe every time you are around your Horse.

Watch carefully to make sure that he is not getting ready to kick at you. If he has one leg cocked back, he may be thinking about it. He will never kick or bite you if you never let him.

You may want to give him space when walking around him so that if he tries, he will miss his kick. If he tries to nibble on your arm, you must say, "No biting" and slap his nose away. Just a light backhand will do. Never hit your Horse very hard if you do. After he is completely bonded with you, he will never think about kicking or biting you again. Brush his whole body, legs, neck and face if needed. You will brush off all debris, mud, then dirt, then dust, from every part of his body.

Keep yourself safe at all time. Brush his mane and for-lock with a detangling brush carefully brushing out all tangles. Some tangles are bad enough that you will need to cut them out. After completing the mane, repeat the process with his tail. In the future, you may be safe brushing his tail and standing directly behind him.

At the beginning we recommend that you stand to one side of his rear and pull his tail over to one side gently while brushing it. Remember that bonding with your Horse can happen quickly or slowly. When choosing your Horse, it works best for all if he seems affectionate to you BEFORE you buy him. That will ensure that the bonding process will occur much more quickly. EVERYTHING that you do with your

Horse at the beginning is part of the bonding process. You are gradually creating a positive, healthy and life-long relationship with your Horse. Please enjoy every minute along the way.

Bathing

You may be tempted to bathe your new best friend often. But keep in mind that his natural oils keep his skin and hair healthy. Too much washing can strip those oils away. Therefore, it is best to bathe your Horse only once a season when it is warm outside. Make sure to buy a quality horse shampoo such as Mane & Tail Shampoo and a washing stall with warm water.

1. Lead your Horse into the washing stall.

2. Now gently tie your Horse's Lead Rope to the hitching rail.

3. Once your Horse is in the washing stall, you can start running the water. Before soaking your Horse, test the water temperature with your fingers carefully. Make sure that it is comfortable, lukewarm water.

4. Get your Horse's entire body wet and begin rubbing in the shampoo to create a gentle lather. Don't use so much that you can't rinse it all out, but also don't use so little that you can't create a rich lather. Try your best to avoid his eyes and mouth. Rinse face as necessary during bathing.

5. Trick: Bathe his head last. This is the part that he may not like.

6. Now rinse him thoroughly using lukewarm water.

Gently work the shampoo out with your hands from top to bottom. Do this several times to get all the shampoo out so his natural oils can get busy keeping him healthy.

7. Now turn the water off and dry him some with a towel. Rub him down thoroughly. Lead him to a dry spot in the sun to let him dry. Keep in mind, at his first chance he will roll in the dirt or the mud directly after he is washed. It is better if he is completely dry before you let that happen.

Hooves

Your Horse needs his hooves to grip, while walking and running. You should clean your Horse's hooves every time that you take him out of the stall. You would have learned at your lessons how to use a hoof pick to scrape out the mud, manure, and other debris stuck in the hooves. It is important as small pieces of gravel can get stuck and cause injury to your horse. Pick up each foot individually and clean each hoof.

Most horses need to have their hooves trimmed approximately every 6-8 weeks. You can learn to do this with a trimmer and a file, or you can hire a Farrier to come and trim for you. The trimmer looks like a cross between giant pliers and a nail clipper. The file is a very large rough file. After trimming ¼ to ½ inch most times the hoof can be filed smooth with just a few strokes. Do not try to trim too short or the hoof will begin to bleed. Some owners decide to have shoes on their horse every time after trimming.

Some horses have very hard hooves and have no problems going anywhere without shoes. Others have difficulty if walking through sharp gravel or rocks. Another option is strap on shoes. These can be put on when needed or taken off when no need. You may decide to only have shoes on the front two feet. This is often enough as a Horse will carry most of his weight on the front feet.

It is recommended that a Farrier at least trim your horse the first time. Please pay close attention to the trimming if you plan to trim yourself in the future. Farriers are not cheap. It is said, "If you want to have a small fortune after owning horses for a few years, you need to start with a large fortune." And another saying, "The human brain is the most amazing organ in the human body, it thinks and works well constantly from before you are born 24/7 and 365 days per year, until you fall in love with a horse." So, you may consider this a warning as to the expense you will pay for your horse over its lifetime.

We predict that for you while reading this book, it is already too late. You are already in love with your horse, or you are already in love with the idea of buying your first Horse. Either way, it is likely too late for any warnings. I have mentioned also that Horses can be dangerous. Usually the deaths occur by accident and the Horse did not mean to kill the person, but it is estimated that 100 deaths per year occur in the United States by horse Riding or handling. It is estimated that 1000-2000 accidents result in Head Injuries per year where the person survives but is never the same again. We repeat, we recommend that you wear a safety Helmut when riding for this reason.

Your Horse's Teeth

- Horses teeth are adapted to grazing

- In an adult horse, there are 12 incisors at the front of the mouth

- There are 24 teeth adapted for chewing, the premolars and molars

- Stallions and geldings have four additional teeth just behind the incisors, a type of canine teeth called "tushes"

- Some horses, both male and female, will also develop one to four very small vestigial teeth in front of the molars, known as "wolf," teeth

- An estimate of a horse's age can be made from looking at its teeth

- The teeth continue to erupt throughout life and are worn down by grazing

- Horses develop a distinct wear pattern, changes in tooth shape, and changes in the angle at which the chewing surfaces meet

- If a horse's teeth do not have a flat surface to chew food properly the process of their digestion is hindered

- It is a good idea to have their teeth examined regularly but no more than once a year

- Most Vets will recommend having your Horse's teeth floated approximately every 1-4 years but most likely by 10 years of age

- Floating your horse's teeth is a process when all the sharp edges and points are filed flat to make an even chewing surface

- More money and expenses for your budget!

Eyes
- Horses have the largest eyes of any land mammal

- Horses have a range of vision of more than 350°

- Horses have excellent day and night vision

- Horses are partially color blind somewhat like red-green color blindness in humans

Your Horse's eyes should be checked by your Vet on a regular basis. You should check your Horse's eyes daily. You should check his stall and paddock on a regular basis and remove any sharp or pointed items such as nails working loose or screw points coming through a surface.

Also look for loose pointed wires or splinters and remove. The reason is your Horse is in danger of piercing one of his eyes. On one of your daily checks you may notice your Horse has one eye that is nearly swollen shut. It is possible your Horse simply got some dust, dirt or small piece of grass in his eye. Before you call the Vet, you should try a product called, "Vetericyn" Ophthalmic Gel for irritated eyes. Wash your hands and then squeeze a thick line of the gel on your finger and put it just above his lower eyelid. He will probably try to pull away from you but hold on and let him rub his eye on the palm of your hand. He will want to do that because his eye is itchy, and it feels good to him. This will help to spread the gel around the surface of his eyeball.

If the swelling does not go down in 24-hours, then you may decide to call your Vet for a stable visit. Some horses go blind in one eye and are still able to be ridden and perform most things successfully. Some horses go completely blind and may be able to be ridden in light terrain if no chance of tripping. That would only occur in a very strong horse/rider relationship of a lifetime. The purpose of this book really is to teach you how to build, nurture and develop that same kind of lifetime relationship.

The horse has a life expectancy of 25 to 30 years. Some Horses live into their 40s and, occasionally, beyond. One horse was said to have lived 62 years in the 19th century. A pony is recorded to have died in 2007 at age 56. Although most of your love will develop with your Horse in the first year, the love and relationship will continue to grow every year that you spend with him. I always liked to hug my Horse around the base of his neck, rub my face against his neck and smell his scent, and hold my chest against his. I first did this with him before I purchased him to be sure he was an affectionate Horse to build a relationship with.

Vet Checks with Your Horse

Every time I obtain a new horse, I will have a Vet check before I commit to that horse. After that I generally won't have another check until I notice some health concern or within 1-4 years whichever comes first. Each time the Vet comes I want him to check his eyes, teeth, hooves, and weight. In addition to properly feeding and exercising your Horse, other aspects of general care are needed to keep your horse healthy throughout his or her life. These include routine veterinary care for vaccinations, parasite control, and dental care; grooming and hoof care; and protection from the elements. A good Vet will offer suggestions for care including medications and feeding. Geriatric horses (older than 20 years old) should see their veterinarian up to twice a year or more frequently because illness is more common in older animals and it can be identified sooner.

Your veterinarian may recommend a wellness program for your horse, including routine blood tests. All my horses are over 20 years old and I have owned them for 10 years. My stables are more like a retirement home for my best friends! Only one of the 3 can be ridden currently, but I intend to make the best life for them possible. They are fortunate and happy horses who live in little piece of paradise.

Health Problems with Your Horse

Most health problems will develop after the age of 20, but many things can happen even before that age. Most Horses suffer from injury or accident before they develop any health problems. In California, Thoroughbred Horses suffered an injury .35% of every race they were involved in.

- Thoroughbred Horses are prone to bleeding from the lungs due to heavy exercise

- Some 10% have low fertility

- Some 5% have abnormally small hearts
- Some have smaller hooves with thin soles and walls, and a lack of cartilage mass (often contributes to foot soreness and lameness)

Other Conditions for Horses:

- Tetanus
- Strangles (Distemper)
- Influenza
- Rhinopneumonitis
- Equine Encephalomyelitis
- Rabies
- Intestinal worms
- Colic
- Laminitis
- Unfortunately, there are many more health conditions can occur with injury or accidents.

Your Vet will also check for these conditions if any symptoms are present. Many Horse owners will make the tough decision to euthanize their horse if the animal is suffering daily and very little chance of recovery. This is a decision of Love that your Horse cannot make for himself. There are times a Vet may tell you of a 10% chance of recovery if you can afford to spend $5000.00 or more for a hospital stay and treatment. Some Horse owners do not have that much money to spend on a 10% chance. If you purchase a Horse who is 5-6 years old and very healthy, you may never experience any health problems until he is well into his 20s. It is common you may continue to ride your horse until he is nearly 30 years old and beyond.

If you live in an area where the temperature drops into the 20- and 30-degree range, you may decide to put a blanket on your horse for those chilly nights. Things to consider include; does your Horse grow a very long winter coat, and would it make you feel better to have him wear a coat? Either way, a blanket will help to keep your Horse warm and dry overnight.

Another consideration is your Horse's water trough in the winter. Many stables have a plug-in heater can be installed in the trough in the winter. A plug-in heater will guarantee that the water never freezes. If no electricity is available, then your Horse will likely poke his nose through the ice for access to water during the night. In the morning you can remove the ice, (and if you have access to water during the freeze) then refill the trough. It can get tricky managing the ice and running water during the cold season.

Mentally Stimulating Activities

Some horses will play with (or be taught to play with) a large inflated ball sometimes will be marked like a soccer ball. If you purchase one and put it in your Horse's paddock, he may play with it on his own. If he seems uninterested you can later work, it into his round pen training and he may develop an interest later. You can also hang a ball in his stall to play with.

Horses can be used for many activities and even competitions if desired. Some horses are known for their long-distance speed abilities and are often used in competitions for racing. Rodeo events are more often participated with Quarter Horses, but some riders choose another horse for barrel racing. Hunter/jumper events typically use other breeds, but some riders choose a Thoroughbred for these events.

Arabian Horses make excellent show horses and are often considered the most beautiful horse in the event. Many horses make excellent trail horses and are willing to take you many miles in a single day. Your Horse may take you all day long if you choose. We will talk more about other mentally stimulating activities later in this book.

Chapter 5

The Horse Stall and Paddock

It is preferred if you can keep your Horse in a horse stall with a paddock. Technically, it is not a horse stall but more properly called a horse shelter. A stall is typically at least 12x12 feet in dimensions and is closed on all four walls with a door closed to keep the horse in at least overnight. A horse shelter is closed on 3 sides and the fourth side is open so that the horse can go in or out at any time.

The shelter may have an access door to bring your Horse in or out and to feed your Horse twice daily. My shelters have a split half door where we can keep the top open more like a window for your Horse to peek out often. The top open also gives access for feeding. We close the top door at night when the weather is expected to be challenging.

I can reach the hay rack to the right of the door and the grain feeder is attached on the inside of the shelter bottom door. That way I can place a flake or two of hay in the rack and dump a small bucket of grain in his feeder without opening the bottom door. One Horse needs a hay bag to reduce the hay that he drops on the floor. The bag can also be reached from the front window for easy feeding.

The shelters are 12x12 feet in dimension. The paddocks should be at least 25x50 feet or larger. If you don't own a horse property and are boarding your horse at a facility or small stables, then you may need to shop around a bit for the right living environment for your Horse. We do not recommend a stall with turnout daily unless your goal is a Show horse.

If you decide on a full-time pasture horse, then we recommend that your Horse have a shelter in the pasture. If you have your Horse on your own property, then you will be required to pick up the paddocks manure on a regular basis. You may decide to have a hired hand clean the paddocks and do minor repairs around your property. If you are cleaning the paddocks yourself, we recommend that you do it daily or at least every other day. The reason for this is the more often you do it the less work it is, and your horse will have less flies and parasites to contend with.

I have cleaned paddocks in the winter with snow after 7 days. Each paddock was a full wheel barrel of manure. If weather does not allow cleaning, you will have a big job ahead. That is why we recommend daily cleaning whenever possible. The manure should be stored in a manure bin until it turns into fertilizer. The fertilizer can be spread over your pastures or you can sell it for $10.00 per truck load. It can also be used in gardens. If you own a horse stables, you can either buy or rent a tractor with a front-end loader and mower with it. You can use the tractor to mow your pastures at least twice per year when the weeds come up. You can use the front-end loader to stir your manure pile once per month.

You can use the front-end loader to spread your fertilizer twice per year. You may also need a harrow to help spread the manure in the pasture. These are some of the advantages of boarding your horse in a nearby stable. You simply pay your monthly board fees. The stable owner is responsible for feeding, cleaning manure, buying a tractor and implements, and all the general farm maintenance.

There is also a provision in the contract the owner will notify you immediately if health concerns arise. You should also give the stable owner the phone number for your Vet for emergencies. If you only have one Horse and the cost in your area is $400 - $500, it is really a pretty good deal. And you end up with more time to spend in direct contact with your new best friend!

Why a horse stall and paddock work best

A horse stall and paddock generally work best for Horses. With a horse stall and paddock, your Horse can be inside or outside at will. He feels more freedom even though he is locked in the paddock overnight every night. You will have complete control what time you let your Horse out and what time you bring him in. In the late spring and early

47

summer, you will have the high growth season for grass.

As mentioned earlier, a Horse can founder from too much sugar content in the grass. The founder can develop into laminitis and could kill your Horse. An affected horse will often be euthanized and is a very painful experience.

During the high growth season, we only leave our horses out for 2-3 hours per day. During the fall, winter and spring we get a lot of rain. The rain puddles up and the pasture is not fit for horses. We limit the grazing to 1-2 hours per day and somedays we do not let them out at all.

Most other days when the conditions are right, we may let them out 10 hours per day or more. The reasons I try to let them out if possible, are that they are getting exercise the whole time they are grazing, and they are eating about 1 pound of grass per hour. If they are out 10 hours, then I only need to feed the horses about 10 pounds of hay that night. So, it is a win-win situation.

Your Horse always prefers fresh pasture grass over hay, and they always prefer to graze and exercise. Your Horse grazing all day will walk approximately 8 miles each day while grazing. And you save money on your hay expenses. Your Horse will eat 7300 pounds of grass or hay each year. If you buy the 3-string bales at 110 pounds each, and you fed him hay only with no pasture grass, it would amount to 65 bales of hay just for one horse. You can buy a whole semi-trailer full of hay each year at a pretty good price per bale. Or, you can buy bales individually 10-20 bales at a time.

We pay almost $23.00 per bale for 3-string Orchard Grass here at my location. At that price, the hay alone costs over $100.00 per month for each horse. The vitamins are 30 pounds per month per horse. The bags of vitamins are 50-pounds and will last one horse 50 days at $23.00 per bag. The COB (corn, oats, and barley) is much less expensive at $12.00 for 50 pounds. One bag of COB will last one horse for about a month.

Horse treats are in 20-pound bags and one bag will last one horse about 3 months at $12.00 per bag. As you can see the expenses rise when your horse gets less time in the pasture. These are more advantages of boarding your horse. But whatever you decide, boarding or owning a horse property, a paddock with a shelter and daily pasture time is what you and your Horse would prefer best.

Allow a few days for your Horse to get used to the Stall. When you bring your Horse to his new home, it will feel like a strange place to him. Most Horses are happiest when they have a pasture pal. Another horse that is in the connecting paddock will provide your horse with a companion to share the pasture with him at turnout time. The stalls are often connected but separate. During the night neither horse will feel lonely as they can often hear each other breathe, snort, or whinny in the connected stall.

After your Horse gets used to his pasture pal and his paddock for 2-3 days, it is a good time to begin building your relationship with your horse. The first day, simply put on his halter and thoroughly brush him. Walk him around a little and then return him to his paddock. The second day you can repeat the process, but saddle him up and put on his bridle, then walk him around a bit. Each day that you work with him, gradually increase your activities with him. Do not try to ride him for about a week of warm up activities.

Picking the Perfect living space for your Horse

We have covered much of this previously, but it is very important to have the right home and environment for your horse. We have covered why it is important to have your horse in a paddock with a shelter and a pasture pal to keep him company when he is turned out in the pasture almost daily.

If you own your horse property, you will have much more control of your Horse's well-being. If you are boarding your Horse, you may have to pick the best place but is not quite perfect. You may not have many options to choose from. There may be only 2-3 stables close to your home. You may take your Horse to one location and a month later move him to your second option for various reasons. The factors of care, feeding, pasture pal, your ability to communicate with the stable owner, and shelter must be taken into consideration.

If your Horse is an "Alpha" gelding and his pasture pal is also an Alpha, then you may move him to a new location due to the two horses fighting. If you are boarding, it is important that you have an even relationship with the stable owner. You should not hesitate to suggest that he find another horse that your Horse can get along with. If a better pasture pal can be located, then you will not have to move your Horse again. Too many moves too often can be traumatic for a young Horse.

Where to Board Your Horse

If you do not own a horse property, then you will have no other options but to board your Horse. It is common that a horse owner will decide to buy a second horse and later a third. If you are boarding, the financial considerations quickly become a factor. If you are paying over $1000.00 and up to $1500.00 per month in boarding costs, and you are paying $1200.00 per month for rent or a house payment, you may start to consider purchasing a small stable for your horses and you to live at instead of boarding. If you research and find that a mortgage for a 5-acre horse ranch and a 3-bedroom home is around $1900.00, then you may consider it less expensive than boarding. You would even have enough money for feed and some maintenance costs. Please don't forget to factor in all the time required for maintenance. If you are working 40 hours per week and can work with your horses 20 hours per week, your time will be considerably hampered with general maintenance of the ranch. The additional time will often come out of the time you could have spent with your horses.

Furnishing the stall

There are not many furnishings in a stall or shelter. They are often hard packed dirt and gravel and can be uncomfortable on your horse's feet. The shelter can be furnished with stall mats to provide an inch of padding. The stall mats are rubber and generally are 4x6 feet dimensions. Most shelter floors can be covered by 6 mats. The shelter should also have a hay rack to keep most of the hay from piling up on the floor. Some horses will make a mess of the hay if it is kept in a rack. Those horses may require a hay bag to reduce the amount of hay wasted on the floor. The net like bag will reduce the amount of hay on the floor. They will only eat the hay from the floor until it gets wet, muddy, dirty, manure or pee on it. When the hay gets dirty it must be thrown away. You can recycle the hay somewhat by using it to fill a muddy area or a puddle. A hay bag will help reduce wasted hay with certain horses. It is also helpful if you have a grain feeder to avoid wasted grain. The hay rack and the grain feeder should be placed so that your horse can be fed without entering his stall each time. The same should be said if using a hay bag. You can hang the hay bag in the stall with hook to clip onto a ring installed right inside the door. It is a good idea to have a horse trough with clean fresh water shared between 2 horses in the connected paddocks. The horse shelters may need some maintenance if a windstorm knocks off some shingles or the paint starts to peal. Some horses like to play with a large inflated ball on rope in his stall. All horses will require a salt lick in the shelter. That is about the extent of furnishing your stall or shelter.

Begin Your Relationship!

As mentioned earlier, every contact and activity that you have with your Horse is about building your relationship. Talk to your Horse often with every contact and activity. Tell him your thoughts and comments about every contact. Hug him daily around the neck for at least 30-seconds. Press your face into his neck and smell his scent. Press your chest against his. He may be a little surprised the first time that you do this. He may even try to step back away from you the first few times. Don't let go when he steps back. Step forward with him and hold on for your 30-seconds. It won't take long before your Horse will begin to enjoy your hugs also. Give him commands while speaking to him as needed. When you put on his halter and start to lead him out of his stall, say, "Walk", and make sure that he walks behind you when coming through the stall door. When you tie him to the hitching rail, to brush him, say, "Stand," then say, "Good Boy," every time he does as he was told.

Proper Handling

Your safety is the primary focus when handling your Horse. I will repeat, if you do not know how to handle and ride a horse, you will need a few lessons before participating with these book instructions. You may need to learn how to put on a halter, saddle and bridle. You need to learn how to pick up each hoof and use a hoof pick to clean the bottom of each hoof thoroughly. You need to know how to halter your horse to lead out of the stall every day that you work with him. You need to pay attention when handling your Horse. If a dog runs up and startles your Horse, he may react dangerously. He may try to run, kick, or even rear up in defense. If you are not prepared and paying attention, you could be dragged, kicked or trampled. A Horse can accidentally kill a human after being startled. To avoid such an outcome, you may need to get out of the way or even let go of his lead rope to keep safe. It is helpful to speak to your Horse often in a very calm, and soothing voice. This will help keep your Horse from reacting as violently when he is startled.

Your Horse will learn not to be startled by as many stimuli. He will likely get used to a dog. If you must walk by a herd of Llamas on your way down a trail, he may be startled if he never saw that kind of animal before. He may freeze and stare for 10-seconds and snort loudly with every exhale. Just calmly speak to him while stroking his neck. Tell him they are not going to hurt him ever. Tell him he is a good boy and squeeze his ribs with your legs saying, "Walk," then calmly walk by. By the third time walking past the Llamas he will likely not react again. In the beginning it is helpful to talk to your Horse constantly always soothing. When handling your Horse, he will face and overcome most of his fears quickly if you are speaking constantly soothing his fears.

Chapter 6

Bad Horse habits

No Biting

Most horses may try to nibble you with their lips. This can be a sign of affection with no intent to harm. It is more like a kiss, a lick, or a taste but no harm if he does not use his teeth. Be careful with this as the horse could try to bite you with his teeth. This might happen at the beginning and before your trust has been built with your Horse and before your Horse has totally fallen in Love with you. After that, it is not as much of a concern. It is important that you not let any biting happen in the beginning. Your goal should be to never get bit or hurt in any way by your Horse. After your Horse falls in love with you, he will never TRY to hurt you in any way.

Easy on The Nibbles

If your Horse becomes close with his pasture mate, you may notice them standing side by side and facing opposite directions. Then you notice they are grooming each other with their teeth on their backs. If your Horse tried to do that with you, you would get hurt in the process. It is probably safer to detour your Horse from nibbling on you in any way in the beginning. As your relationship grows you may decide your trust can allow a few nibbles and kisses.

But always go easy on the nibbles because you can accidentally be bit by your Horse. I have seen the results of horse bites and it will usually result in bruising and/or blood. Horses can be dangerous creatures!

No Kicking

A kick from your Horse can result in severe head injury, bruises, broken ribs and other bones, and even death. A kick can be intentional or accidental. The intentional kicks will most often occur during the beginning of your relationship and typically up to one year for a slow built relationship. After that, an accidental kick is more likely. If you never put yourself in a position to be kicked during your first year, it is likely that your Horse will never kick you on purpose. If you learn that your Horse kicks at dogs and other horses, then you know to be extra careful when dogs or other horses are nearby.

You will know that if a dog or another horse is nearby that the dreaded accidental kick can occur. This can occur when your Horse may think he is trying to kick the dog or horse but accidentally kicks you instead. These accidental kicks can be just as bad or worse than an intentional kick. If you know that your Horse will kick at a horse fly, bee, or wasp, then the same caution should occur if you notice a nagging insect around your Horse.

If you know that your Horse may try to kick at a stranger, then warn the stranger to stay to the side or in front of the Horse, and again handle your Horse with the same caution. Exercise caution with any other things that your Horse may try to kick at but could accidentally kick you. When you are looking to purchase your new Horse, you will often notice in the advertisement that this horse does not kick or bite. That is a good start to look at. The ad may also say "easy keeper". Easy keeper means that they do not require as much hay as most horses. It may also say "husband safe." Husband safe can mean two things; the horse likes males and females alike, and/or the horse can be ridden by a beginner. These are all important considerations. If you are not sure of the horse for sale, then you can ask for a free care lease or a 3-month free trial to make sure the horse is a good fit. These allow you to try out the Horse for a period to make sure that you want this horse to be your best friend. If it does not work out, you can return the horse to the original owner and start shopping for another horse. This is highly recommended.

No Stepping on Your Feet

If you allow your Horse to step on your foot, it is very likely to result in broken bones and/or bruising. This is another event that can be intentional or accidental. The intentional stepping will only occur during the beginning of your relationship and typically up to one year for a slow built relationship. After that, an accidental stepping is more likely. If you never put yourself in a position to be stepped on during your first year, it is likely that your Horse will never step on your feet on purpose. When you hug your Horse every day, he could accidentally or intentionally step on your feet. It is easy to keep your feet safe while hugging your Horse. Keep some space between your feet and his hooves. If your Horse moves during the hug you should adjust your feet accordingly. Exercise the same caution every time your feet are near his hooves in the front or the back.

No Rubbing it's Face on Your Body

This is not generally considered a sign of aggression, but more accurately, your Horse has an itchy face and wants to use you as a scratching post. This can even be described as a sign of affection; however, your Horse can hurt you or knock you down when rubbing his face on you. A good solution, when you notice your Horse is about to rub his face on you, to step back and allow him to use your hands as his scratching post. He will quickly learn this is an efficient alternative way to get his itch scratched. This will satisfy your Horse and will keep you safe.

No Chasing

After you have given your Horse a few days to get acclimated to his surroundings, and you decide to put his halter on and take him out to brush him, it is advised to take him out before he is turned out in his pasture for the day. It is much easier to catch your Horse inside the paddock than from out of the pasture. If you decide to take out your Horse after he is already in the pasture, you may find that he does not want to go with you. He still does not know you yet. He may run away from you as you walk towards him. Never chase your Horse to try to catch him in the pasture. It can quickly become a game to him and then be hard to change later. Do not chase him even once. If he runs away from you turn around and go, get some grain in a bucket. Walk out towards him again shaking the bucket as bait. A Horse would often walk towards you to get some of the grain offered to him. If he still does not come, then wait until he is in the paddock before you put a halter on him. In time, your Horse will always come to you from the pasture with a whistle, call his name, or offer him a treat. But, never chase your Horse.

No Running Away

At the beginning of your relationship with your Horse, he may run away from you or try to run away. This is another no/no, but as mentioned above, do not chase your Horse if he gets away from you. If you are near another horse that will come to you, then it is likely your Horse will soon follow when he sees the other horse getting some treats or grain. If he still does not come, then wait until he is in the paddock before you put a halter on him. In time, your Horse will never run away and always come to you from the pasture with a whistle, call his name, or offer him a treat.

No Aggression

Aggression can come in the form of kicking, biting, smashing your foot, smashing you between the horse and a wall, and butting you under the chin with his head. If the Horse is still aggressive after a week, you should consider a replacement. Aggression is a perfect reason to ask for a free trial period or free care lease so that you are not required to sell the horse to another owner and then find a new Horse.

You should be able to tell if the horse likes you or not before bringing him home. Some aggression can occur if your Horse is not happy with his new environment. It is possible that the Horse does not like his pasture mate. It is possible, (when boarding your horse) that he does not like the person who feeds him.

It is possible that he does not like the children or dogs that he is exposed to when you are not around. You may not determine what, is the cause of his behavior. If the Horse is still aggressive after a week, you should consider a replacement. It is recommended that you ask for a free trial period or free care lease. Another reason for the free period is that it is hard to sell a horse that you do not like for some reason. When you have a free trial period, it will not be your responsibility to sell the horse before you can find your replacement. Many horse riders are easily discouraged when trying to sell a horse with known faults.

There is to be no aggression from you towards your Horse. A light slap on the nose or the neck is not considered aggression if you do not deliver a hard or stinging smack. A light slap is merely a means of getting your Horse's attention if he is nibbling too much or if he starts to squeeze you against the wall. Never whip, punch with closed fist, or kick your Horse. This kind of aggression can permanently traumatize your Horse and could potentially damage your relationship beyond repair. If you are worried about a light slap you can practice "patting" him lightly when you are petting, stroking and brushing him. Do it affectionately as practice so that you can see that a light slap is only meant to get his attention and will not traumatize him in any way. When you give him a smack for a good reason, you should say, "hey stop" at the same time to add some verbal communication to your body language slap.

Non-aggressive Training

Every aspect of your training is to be totally non-aggressive from the very beginning. Most of your training will be body language to your horse, accompanied with verbal commands at the same time. In the past, most horses were literally "broke" during their training. A cowboy would tie the horse to a post in the center of the corral and put a blanket on him, saddle on him, and then insert his bit and reins around his neck. He would then mount the horse with no time to get used to anything. The horse, being so scared, would begin to buck, hop, and rear up trying to throw this rider off his back. The cowboy having experience at this kind of thing, would likely ride him out until the horse was so exhausted that he would simply submit and quit fighting. And then the horse was broke. This did not inspire any kind of love, trust, or desire to please. Instead the horse was left with dislike, fear and a desire to get away or escape.

Today most horses are saddle broke in a much more, kind, patient, and gradual method. When a young filly or colt is a few weeks old, the owner will gently and kindly put on his halter for the first time. The young horse will be led around on a regular basis during his first year. He will be handled and brushed on a regular basis. He will be weaned from his Mother and gradually learn to love and trust his human friends. He may have a saddle blanket put on him to get used to gradually. When the weather turns colder and drops below freezing, it is recommended that the young horse be provided with a blanket for warmth that is strapped

63

on in the afternoon prior to the anticipated freezing temperatures. After the first year, you can try a saddle on him a few times on a regular basis. He can be led around to get used to the saddle. He is not to be ridden until he passes 2-3-years of age. Before riding him, the trainer will lay across him on the saddle a few times to get him used to having weight on him. The horse will see other horses being ridden by a human during his first few years. After a few days of having weight on him, the trainer will attempt the first ride. If there has been love, respect and honor bestowed on the horse, then there is likely to be no bucking, hopping or rearing up. The horse has gradually been saddle-broken and is essentially (saddle) broke before he is ridden for the first time. That is the essence of non-aggressive training.

Things to Consider

As mentioned before, the horse is a prey animal, and humans are considered predators. The cowboy of the past did not realize how the horse felt when he roped a wild horse from the herd and tied to the post, put blanket, saddle and reins on the horse. He did not realize when he climbed up on the saddle that the horse thought he had a predator on his back. The cowboy did not realize the horse was filled with fear and anxiety. The horse thought he was going to be killed. The horse felt he needed to do everything that he could to get this predator off his back, to survive and to get back to the safety of his herd. The cowboy did not realize that this way of breaking a horse, would inspire distrust and fear of humans that might never change throughout his life. The cowboy may have never considered that you might be able to call a horse and have him walk right up to you. The cowboy was accustomed to having to ride out and rope horses to saddle, because they would not come to if you called them. It would take years of a gentle relationship before a horse could come to love or trust his new owner.

Chapter 7

How the Training Works

The training works by developing a relationship of love and trust before the horse is broke and with every new owner before his relationship training is completed. When the horse loves and trusts you, he will want to please you, and keep you safe. When a horse wants to please you, he will strive to do as instructed without delay or question. The relationship training works when conducted on a slow, patient and gradual process. After every step, gradually introduce your next training phase. Every step of the process should be done with love, encouragement, and respect. Always say, "Good boy" every time he does another command correctly. Give him treats often (in the beginning) after his success. Stroke him on the neck and give him daily hugs. As he gets used to these things his love and respect for you will grow daily.

How to Perform Training

It is important that you do not approach your horse if you are feeling any kinds of anger, fear or anxiety. Some people may need to meditate for a few minutes prior to working with your horse to dispel any unwanted feelings. Your horse can sense these kinds of feelings and will not perform as well. He will be distracted by your feelings. You should approach your horse when you are feeling love, respect, and confidence. The training is really all about body language. All body language should be accompanied by verbal commands. Your horse can read expressions on your face. He can read your posture and stance. He can read your hand signals. He can read every combination of all three at the same time. Any Variation of the three can mean something different to a well-trained horse.

Good Performance Rewards!

Your Horse should be acknowledged for every correct behavior he achieves during training. Every time you should say, "Good Boy" at the very least. That is a reward. When he has an ah ha moment and gets a new understanding in the process, you should still say, "Good Boy," but might also stop him and give him a treat and give him a hug. All three are considered rewards. You will give him more rewards at the beginning than later. After he learns a desired behavior, then that is what is expected from him every time in the future. He will not be rewarded for the same behavior repeatedly. A simple "Good Boy" is enough for all future repeated behaviors. It is a reward when you feed him, brush him, train him, exercise him, let him out to pasture, hug him, and talk to him. Every activity is considered a reward for having good behavior only. If he has some bad behavior during one of your activities, then you may decide to skip a day for the bad behavior. Taking away one of his rewards for a day is the only kind of punishment you will do to your horse. Often, after skipping a day, the horse will be on his best behavior in the activity. An example: your horse is fidgeting around too much while you are brushing him, so you skip the next day. The horse will likely stand very still, while he is being brushed a day later.

When to Start Training

Guess what? If you already have your Horse and have spent any time with him at all, you have begun your training. Every connection with your horse is considered training. If you don't have your Horse yet, then you should begin your training as soon as you get your horse. As soon as you begin interacting with your Horse, his training has begun. Remember, what you are really training your Horse, is how to love you, honor and respect you. That is all really. Every hand signal or command has everything to do with love. At the same time, you are learning to love, honor and respect your Horse. There are no mistakes. Only learning opportunities. Your Horse will learn how to be trained by you and you will learn how to train your Horse. Every Horse is unique and an individual. Every human is unique and individual. Some of the items of training coming up may not suit you or your Horse, and you will likely develop a slightly modified form of communication with your Horse unique and specific to you and your Horse.

Positive Reinforcement Not Punishment

As previously mentioned, you will reward your Horse every time he is performing correct behavior. Always say, "Good Boy." Always pet him and hug him. Always talk to him. These are all considered positive reinforcement or rewards. We are going to learn about a long whip on a long fiberglass rod. You will never strike the horse with the whip. You will learn to whip the ground behind him as a form of communication. Never punish your horse with any form of physical violence. When you feel that your Horse needs punishment, you will simply skip the activity for a day as punishment. There is no kind of physical violence involved with that kind of punishment. You don't need to call skipping a day punishment, instead you can call it giving your Horse a break for a day. If you have another horse you can work with, where your Horse can see you, it can be helpful to perform the activity with another horse. This can inspire your Horse to behave properly the next day. Your Horse may even feel a tinge of jealousy. Always adjust accordingly to your Horse's unique personality.

Consistency is Key

It is important to keep your Horse on the same schedule and keep all activities the same each time. Your Horse should be fed at approximately the same times each day, morning and evening. You should clean his manure at the same time. You should add fresh water to his trough on every other day schedule or every third day. You should empty and scrub out his trough every 2-3 weeks. Do not let the trough get too much algae, dirt, grass, water bugs, and for sure do not let any mosquito larvae hatch. The mosquitos will bother you and your Horse. Be consistent with every aspect of your training. Always give a consistent amount of love and affection every day that you interact with your Horse.

When you change a schedule try to do it gradually. For instance, if you feed every morning one hour after sunrise and every evening one hour before sunset, that will gradually change as the times change through-out the year. Your Horse will never likely see that as a change as the days get longer or shorter. To your Horse, it will seem like there was no changes at all. Every other change should be conducted in a gradual manner to stay consistent. Your Horse will thrive and appreciate your consistence.

Secrets of Round Pen Training

No secrets really. The main advantage is not a secret to many horse enthusiasts. The main advantage is that you will not have to use a long rope after your Horse understands his commands. Your Horse may have already been trained in the round pen and may already know all his commands. Either way, it is recommended that you have him on a long rope in the round pen for at least the first time. After you are certain that your Horse knows all his commands, the next time you can let him off his lead rope in the round pen and give him his commands without a rope. At that point, your Horse should go around the perimeter of the round pen, "walk, trot, canter, etc."

Secrets to Long Lead Training your Horse

If your Horse does not already understand round pen or long lead training, then it will take a bit longer and require patience and excellent communication with your Horse. This is the time when you will really learn to communicate with your Horse.

Chapter 8

Basic Horse Commands

The basic Horse Commands are:

Come

At this time, it is likely that you have had your Horse for 2-3 weeks. If you were able to feed him every evening, then you would have had the opportunity to teach your Horse to come in from the pasture in the evening when you called him in. When calling him in, teach him to come to his name, teach him to come to a whistle, and teach him to come to body language. These will be easy to teach to him if he has a pasture mate who was already trained to come in the evening for feeding. It is likely your Horse will follow his pasture mate the first day, and common that your Horse would come in first on the second day. After that you can practice each of the above methods on alternating days to allow equal practice to each method. First day call his name. Give him time to see you before you call his name. When he comes in tell him, "Good Boy," and give him a treat. The second day, when you walk out whistle to your Horse, but only after he has a chance to see you again. When he comes in tell him, "Good Boy," and give him a treat. The third day walk out to the gate until he looks at you, and without saying anything, spread your arms wide as if you want to give him a hug and hold that position until he begins to walk towards you. You may decide to use a different hand signal. That should be fine if it gets his attention and he comes in. When he comes in tell him, "Good Boy," and give him a treat. After the three days and if all days were successful, you can probably stop giving him a treat and simply say, "Good Boy," when he comes in. And from that point on it is common your Horse will come in from the pasture as soon as he sees you. You will not even have to call his name. Your presence near his gate is what is telling him to come.

Stand

You will begin teaching your Horse this command directly after his 3-day acclimation period. The fourth day after you go into your Horse's paddock to halter him, walk up to him and give him a treat and say, "Stand." Then immediately put his halter on and lead him out of his shelter to the hitching rail. I must repeat here, if you have not yet learned to halter a horse, then you will need to take a few horseback riding lessons and be sure to include training for horse handling, saddling, and grooming. It is important that you know how to do all those things before working with your Horse. After you bring him to the hitching rail, tie his lead rope leaving your Horse a little slack to move around some. If you tie your lead rope tight, it may be fearful to your Horse and cause him to resist. After you have him tied tell him, "Stand." Begin to brush your Horse. If he starts to fidget or try to reach for some grass, then give a firm tug on his rope and tell him again, "Stand." After a few repetitions, it is likely your Horse will stop his fidgeting and enjoy his being brushed by you. A very solid connection can be formed in the act of daily brushing of your Horse. Try to make it also like a massage or spa treatment of your Horse. He will recognize this as a reward and usually respond in gratitude. When you recognize his gratitude, you will know at that point that you did choose the right Horse for you. Brush him every time before you work with him. The gratitude will carry over into every step of future training.

Walk

At this time, it is likely that you have had your Horse for 2-3 weeks. You have been calling him in every evening for his feeding. You have been brushing him every day much like a spa treatment. He knows how to come by name, by whistle, and by body language with whatever signal you decided was best. Your Horse has learned how to Stand on command and when you put on his halter, and when he is tied at the hitching rail.

It is recommended that you use a long lead to teach your Horse the command to Walk. You should use a long lead the first few times even when you have access to a round pen. You should also use your long whip (many have a flag attached). The whip is not to punish your Horse ever, but instead just to get him moving. Every time that you lead your Horse somewhere you should say, "Walk," and then begin walking beside your Horse. It is likely that he knows this command by now. Connect your long lead to your Horse's halter and say, "Walk," and then lead him into the round pen or the pasture area where you can work with your Horse without interruption. Find your central location where you will stand, while your Horse moves around in circles around you. Stop in the center and you will likely notice that your Horse stopped as soon as you did, without a command. This means that you have established another connection.

Your Horse has learned on his own, to follow your lead without any verbal commands. It is kind of a big deal to achieve that so soon in your training. Your Horse may have already been trained most of this, but he has not yet learned to do it under your command. From the center point give your Horse a little nudge forward on his lead rope and say, "Walk," and click your tongue as he begins to move away. If he stops or hesitates, then whip the ground with your long whip about five feet behind him on the ground. The reason it is important to whip 5 feet behind him is so that there is no chance that any part of him will be struck by the whip.

Your Horse will be a little scared by the whip and begin walking in a circle around you. You have his long lead in one hand and the long whip in the other. When he begins to walk around you in a large circle tell him, "Good Boy," every time that he is halfway around the circle. If he slows down or stops, you will need to whip the ground 5-feet behind him again repeating, "Walk." Only make him do 3 circles his first day and tell him, "Good Boy," then stop and face him and give him the body language signal for the command Come and say it verbally. He should come into the center of the circle to you and stop directly in front of you. When he comes into you tell him, "Good Boy" several times and stroke his cheek and neck. Even give him one of his favorite treats.

For this example, your Horse went around three times to his left. Now you will have him walk three laps to his right. For this part of the exercise your command will be Walk Right. After your Horse is rewarded again for walking three additional laps to his right, you will teach your Horse to trot for 3 laps in both directions.

Trot

Teaching your Horse to trot is almost the same as teaching him to walk in both directions. (This will be different if you buy a gaited horse such as a Tennessee Walker. Instead of trot, you will ask your

76

gaited horse to do a fast walk or running walk.) The difference for other horses is you will likely have to be more persistent and whip the ground behind him several times before he will break into a trot, but say the command, "Trot Left" and then repeat the command each time that you whip the ground. After he breaks into a trot then repeat, "Good Boy" every half lap until he completes three laps left and then three times right.

You can customize his own training as determined by yourself. For instance, you do not have to call him in to the center after every three laps. You can change your Horse direction from Trot Left to Trot Right without stopping him. Simply say to your Horse, "Trot Right" and point your right arm to your right. If he does not immediately change direction then, whip the ground 10 feet in front of him and repeat the command. If he does not respond the second time, then you will need to step in front of his path and hold your arms out and repeat the command, "Trot Right". That should not be needed but is a last resort on your third try to turn him. The next time you try to turn him he will likely obey on your first request. Tell him, "Good Boy" every half lap.

After your Horse has trotted both directions 3 laps each it is time to teach him to canter on his lead rope. You can call him in first or you can make him switch directions to the left and then encourage him to move past the trot and into a slow canter.

Canter

This command is Canter Left. Repeat the command as you whip the ground 5-feet behind him. Repeat the command as you whip the ground several times until he breaks into a canter left. Tell him, "Good Boy" every half lap. (A reminder that the long whip is approximately 5 feet long and the fiberglass rod is 5 feet long and often has a flag attached).

Use the same signals, commands and body language to turn his canter right for 3 more laps. Tell him, "Good Boy" every half lap. Now, you need to tell him to walk for 3 laps to settle down. He will gladly do that for you after his effort of trot and canter. You have accomplished an important thing with your Horse now. He will never forget his training unless he waits a long time between this activity. After he finishes his 3 laps walking, call him into the center and tell him, "Good Boy" several times and stroke his cheek and neck. Even give him one of his favorite treats.

If you are ready to ride, this would be a good time to ride him for approximately 30 minutes after his long lead and round pen training.

The next time when working with your Horse you should gradually increase his laps from 3 in each direction, to 4 in each direction, then 5, then 6 all the way up to 10 laps in each direction.

After he has completed 10 laps in each direction for walk, trot and canter for 10-12 days together, you can assess when you think his training is completed on the long lead or round pen. You also need to assess if your Horse is better under saddle after his long lead exercise or the same without his exercise in advance of the ride. You can increase the length of time that you ride your Horse also. 30 minutes the first day and then 45 the second day, 1-hour the third day. You can work your Horse all the way up to a 16-hour ride if you desire and have the time. As mentioned earlier, your Horse is made for speed and endurance and can easily carry you all day long after your gradual training and build up to that point.

Easy

It is recommended that you repeat the word, "Easy" repeating it over and over if your Horse seems startled, worried, worked up, or anything but his usual calm and relaxed self. You are telling him to go back to us calm and relaxed state of being. If your Horse is running too fast towards you at feeding time, you can say, "Easy" to slow him down. It is important that you always use your commands at the appropriate times. When you first start training your Horse, you want to repeat his commands often but only as needed.

Chapter 9

Understanding Horse Body Language

Just like you are using body language to communicate with your Horse, your Horse has his own body language to communicate with you and other horses. If your Horse lays back his ears at you, it may mean that he is angry or annoyed at you. Did you take too long to give him his grain? Usually, a few strokes on his neck and he will perk his ears forward again, meaning he was not very angry with you at all. Perhaps he is angry because he has not seen you for over 24-hours? That kind of anger is only momentary and nothing to be concerned with.

When you see two horses facing each other and both have their ears laid back, then they are likely in competition for some reason. Often the reason is simply which horse is in charge at that moment. They may reach out and try to nip each other. They may both turn around and kick towards each other. It is uncommon a horse will get bit or kicked but it can happen. Never allow these kinds of behaviors towards you. If you see your Horse reach out to try to bite you or turn around and face his back end toward you, or even kick towards you. Always get out of the way first, and simultaneously shout, "No" and you can say his name and repeat a few times so that he knows that this type of behavior is never allowed.

You may see your Horse reach over a fence towards another horse on the other side. This can be a challenge to the other horse. If the other horse accepts the challenge, he will reach over the fence also and they will begin to try to nip each other around the face. It is common one horse will bite a small piece of hair from the other horse's face. The spot will remain hairless for months. Discourage this kind of behavior by shouting, "No" using both of their names.

You may notice your Horse and another horse get into an actual fight when they are both kicking each other and landing blows. Again, shout, "No" and use both of their names. Typically, a fight won't last too long and they will go their separate ways. If you notice the same two horses repeatedly fighting daily, it is time to try to find a new pasture mate your Horse will get along with. If your Horse is fighting with another gelding, it is likely he would get along with a mare who is somewhere in the middle of the pecking order.

You may notice your Horse starts to crib on his stall door or a fence rail. Cribbing is when they basically press down with their top row of teeth onto the fence rail. Not quite chewing but will create a worn down look on your rail. Some would say this is a type of compulsive disorder with very little chance of curing. Others would say your Horse is bored and you should take him out of his stall and work with him or ride him. You may notice that your Horse is pacing back and forth in his paddock. Similar kind of behavior in a way. Some would say this is a type of compulsive disorder with very little chance of curing. Others would say your Horse is bored, and you should take him out of his stall and work with him or ride him.

You may notice that your Horse gets very excited at feeding time. This is a very natural response for your Horse. He may run around at full canter and come skidding to a stop, and then take off running again. He may run into his paddock before you even call him in. He may stand in his stall with his head out his window, bobbing his head up and down as if he is saying, "Yes, it is finally feeding time!" He may be speaking to you with the sounds he can make and trying to say the same thing.

You will come to understand your Horse's body language a little at a time. Look for the stimulus to his body language. Was he startled by a different creature? Is he responding to a large horse fly that is pestering his rear? Was he startled by a bird that flew by in front of his face? Is he communicating anger to another horse that has come to investigate? He may be thinking, "What do you want? Mind your own business. This is my time with my Herd-Leader! Get out of here!" After a varied timeframe, you will likely understand the tiniest stiffening of one of his muscles, or a swat of his tail. Every Horse is different but mostly will communicate in a similar way.

Posture

Mostly your Horse will have two important postures. Your Horse will likely stiffen up when he is responding to some stimuli close to him. It may be a bug, a dog, another horse, or even another new human. Your Horse will also have a relaxed posture, when there is nothing near him to bother him in any way. Your Horse will likely learn to relax during most interactions with you. He will relax into the experience of being brushed by you from head to toe.

He will relax when you are scratching and rubbing his sweet spot. It is sometimes hard to find a sweet spot on your Horse. It is generally a spot that they cannot reach with a hoof or their mouth. I have found it is common to be on their neck or throat. When you find the spot, you may notice your Horse gets a far-away look in his eyes as you scratch his neck, pointing his head straight up and suddenly he is about 8-feet tall. Careful not to put him too far into a trance as your Horse can lose his balance and almost fall on you. Careful! Always put your safety first. It is just as important to put yourself into a safe position when you notice that your Horse's posture has stiffened up. He may be about to react to whatever stimuli is bothering him. He may react in a way that could hurt you such as kicking or smashing you against the wall of the stall. He may be about to run away from the perceived danger and could potentially run you down. Put yourself into a safe position immediately and before he reacts. Careful! Always put your safety first.

Tail

Your Horse will likely have a beautiful way of holding his tail up with the hair floating behind as he prances about. Your Horse will hold his tail up in this way for several reasons. He may do it when alarmed by a deer or an elk a quarter mile away which he could see or smell or both. He may hold it up to compete with another gelding nearby, often when a mare is nearby, both horses' hopeful of the mare's attention.

Neither gelding can breed with the mare, but they still both want her favor. Your Horse also will hold his tail up to show off to the human herd-leader (you). If you decide to later learn to show your Horse to win some ribbons, it is likely you would have to run with him in the show ring so that he is trotting. Your Horse will often hold his tail up when trotting. It is a very beautiful form of communication from your Horse.

Face

You will likely laugh often when you are learning your Horse's facial expressions. Your Horse can open his eyes wide with surprise. Your Horse can show you the whites of his eyes in anger or fear. Your Horse can flare his nostrils wide with anger or fear. Your Horse has two responses to anger or fear. Flight or Fight are his two responses. Either response can put you in danger. That is why it is very important for you to understand your Horse's body language and facial expressions.

Your Horse may likely make a very funny expression after you give him a dose of worming medication. They often do not appreciate the flavor and will raise their mouth up and peel back his lips showing all his front teeth. It is a very funny expression then. We talked about when your Horse lays back his ears. That usually signifies anger or impatience. You may notice that your Horse is avoiding eye contact or even no contact at all. You may decide to give your Horse a break from riding or round pen that day. Just brush him and turn him out to the pasture and try again the next day. You will come to understand your Horse's individual facial expressions.

Whinny

When your Horse speaks a whinny to you, it is recommended you either whinny back, or shout, "Hello Mister – ". Your Horse is likely trying to say, "Hello, it is great to see you! Please feed me now." When your Horse's pasture mate is taken out of his paddock, and your Horse is left alone in the paddock, then the other horse is ridden away from the stable towards the trail. You may hear your Horse whinny to his pasture mate, "Where are you going? When are you coming back? I don't want to be alone!" If some strange horses are being ridden by your stables, you may hear your Horse whinny at the horses, "Hello, who are you? Where do you live? I wish I could go with you!" Sometimes you will hear one of the strange horse's whinny back. Who really knows what your Horse is saying? It is fun to guess though.

Snorting

When you notice your Horse was startled by something, he may flare up his nostrils and exhale very loudly like a snort. He may do this a dozen times in a row before he can relax again. If that is his only reaction it is a good idea to say, "Easy, easy, easy big fella" over and over while stroking the side of his neck. This is a good way to help him to relax without reacting further. He may do this generally for fear or anger, but most often fear and being startled.

Squealing

It seems more common for mares to squeal, but a gelding may squeal rarely. It is common if a gelding is bothering the mare in any manner, she will squeal her complaint or protest very loudly. When you notice a mare is about to squeal it is a good idea to step back and maybe even cover your ears because it is piercing and a loud sound that can hurt your ears. Squealing is almost always done out of anger and protest by a mare to a gelding.

Neighing

Neighing is like whinny but a much lower tone and quieter sound. This is generally a sound that your Horse will make while it is feeling relaxed, safe, and possibly ecstatic. Your Horse may make that sound while being brushed, massaged, scratched, or rubbed. We like this sound mostly for what your Horse is trying to communicate. He may be saying, "Thank you, that feels so good, please don't stop, or a little to the right." Neighing is almost always from a feeling of safety and is not out of fear.

Chapter 10

Hand Cues – Pretty Handy!

The only standard hand cues are left and right. All the others you can choose for yourself and your Horse will come to understand them all with a few months of work. After your Horse has learned all his commands and hand cues, then you will work with or ride your Horse simply for exercise as his training is completed.

Stand Hand Cue

Your Horse can be taught the hand signal for stand when you are working with him in the round pen or long lead. You can decide any hand signal that you would prefer. One successful example is to hold your arm out towards your Horse while he is approaching, and then drop your arm to your side and at the same time say, "Stand." After he has completed half of his laps, call him into you and give your command and hand signal simultaneously. Your Horse should learn and know all his hand signals within the first dozen training sessions. Remember all the hand signals are only used for groundwork, training, and exercise. You will not use them when you are riding your Horse. You will only use leg cues, some verbal commands, and reins when riding.

Left Hand Cue

Your Horse can be taught the hand signal for Left when you are working with him in the round pen or long lead. One successful example is to hold your arm out pointing with your left arm to his left while he is moving to his right and say, "Left" simultaneously. If he does not change directions from right to left immediately then you must strike the ground with your long whip in front of him. He will get the message and change directions now moving to his left. Your Horse should learn and know all his hand signals within the first dozen training sessions. Remember all the hand signals are only used for groundwork, training, and exercise. You will not use them when you are riding your Horse. You will only use leg cues, some verbal commands, and reins when riding.

Right Hand Cue

Your Horse can be taught the hand signal for Right when you are working with him in the round pen or long lead. One successful example is to hold your arm out pointing with your right arm to his right while he is moving to his left and say, "Right" simultaneously. If he does not change directions from left to right immediately then you must strike the ground with your long whip in front of him. He will get the message and change directions now moving to his right. Your Horse should learn and know all his hand signals within the first dozen training sessions. Remember all the hand signals are only used for groundwork, training, and exercise. You will not use them when you are riding your Horse. You will only use leg cues, some verbal commands, and reins when riding. When doing your left- and right-hand cue, it is important to have your long whip in the opposite hand and pointing down when you issue the command. You will have to switch the whip to the other hand for one direction.

Walk Hand Cue

Your Horse can be taught the hand signal for Walk when you are working with him in the round pen or long lead. One successful example is to push your hand (use right hand if you want him to go left and left arm to push him right) in the air towards his rear end and tail. When you give your hand signal (with your right arm) you will simultaneously say, "Walk Left" and the first few times you may need to whip the ground behind him to get him moving. Your Horse should learn and know all his hand signals within the first dozen training sessions. Remember all the hand signals are only used for groundwork, training, and exercise. You will not use them when you are riding your Horse. You will only use leg cues, some verbal commands, and reins when riding. For the walk trot, and canter hand signals it is okay if you have the whip in the same hand you are giving the signal for. Your Horse will naturally move away from the whip so either hand is okay.

Trot Hand Cue

Your Horse can be taught the hand signal for Trot when you are working with him in the round pen or long lead. One successful example is to push your hand slightly at a higher level than walk (use right hand if you want him to go left and left arm to push him right) in the air towards his rear end and tail. When you give your hand signal (with your right arm) you will simultaneously say, "Trot Left" and the first few times you may need to whip the ground behind him to get him to break into a trot.

Your Horse should learn and know all his hand signals within the first dozen training sessions. Remember all the hand signals are only used for groundwork, training, and exercise. You will not use them when you are riding your Horse. You will only use leg cues, some verbal commands, and reins when riding. For the walk trot, and canter hand signals it is okay if you have the whip in the same hand you are giving the signal for. Your Horse will naturally move away from the whip so either hand is okay.

Canter Hand Cue

Your Horse can be taught the hand signal for Canter when you are working with him in the round pen or long lead. One successful example is to push your hand slightly at a higher level than trot (use right hand if you want him to go left and left arm to push him right) in the air towards his rear end and tail. When you give your hand signal (with your right arm) you will simultaneously say, "Canter Left" and the first few times you may need to whip the ground behind him to get him to break into a canter.

Your Horse should learn and know all his hand signals within the first dozen training sessions. Remember all the hand signals are only used for groundwork, training, and exercise. You will not use them when you are riding your Horse. You will only use leg cues, some verbal commands, and reins when riding. For the walk trot, and canter hand signals it is okay if you have the whip in the same hand you are giving the signal for. Your Horse will naturally move away from the whip so either hand is okay.

Good Hand Cue

It is recommended that you wait to use this hand signal until he has completed all his exercises and you are calling him into you for rewards. You may choose to give him a short break when he has completed half of his exercises and can use this hand signal then also. For this hand signal, simply bring your open hand or closed fist up from your side and diagonally up to your heart or the center of your chest. You should immediately and simultaneously say, "Good Boy" and call him into you for some rewards. Your Horse should learn and know all his hand signals within the first dozen training sessions. Remember all the hand signals are only used for groundwork, training, and exercise. You will not use them when you are riding your Horse. You will only use leg cues, some verbal commands, and reins when riding.

Chapter 11

Alpha Horse

An Alpha horse is most often an Alpha mare. The only other higher alpha is a stud or stallion male horse. Most male horses are geldings and are not alpha males (some geldings are alpha but rare). Most Horse geldings are middle of the pecking order but rarely would be the "low horse on the totem pole." All the above horses can still be good riding horses, but a loving relationship is needed for most. An Alpha horse may not do as well in the round pen or long lead. For some, they do not take commands well on the ground but can still perform almost perfectly under saddle. It is most likely your Horse will be in the middle of the pecking order.

This kind of Horse will be likely to get along with most horses as a pasture mate. A middle of the pecking order gelding is likely to get along with most geldings and most mares. Watch carefully after the horses are first introduced. A little nipping and kicking towards each other is normal but watch to be sure it is not going to get out of hand. Do not make your Horse endure constant or often abuse from his pasture mate. It is usually best if your horse is in the middle of the pecking order but is probably more important that the Horse seems affectionate to you BEFORE you buy him. If you are not sure, always ask for a temporary free care lease, or trial period of at least 90-days before you commit to a purchase.

How do You Become the Alpha?

It is recommended that you take a moment to inventory your mood, your feelings, and your intentions before you begin to work with your Horse. This is most important at the beginning. It is very important that you are feeling happy, content, focused, confident, and bold. Your Horse will notice if you are feeling depressed, anxiety, fear, or low self-esteem.

To become the Alpha in your relationship with your Horse, you must present as confident, bold, happy, content, and always in charge of every moment and action. You should stand with erect posture. You should keep your shoulders back, chest out, and straight spine. All verbal commands should be clear, concise, and firm.

If your Horse reaches down to munch some grass while you are leading him, give him a quick ("check") or tug on his lead rope to keep him moving in the right direction. If he looks around in another direction, give him a quick tug. Direct him to move straight to the destination. Always stay in charge when you are working with him.

Never give your Horse any corrections in Anger when there is a chance you may correct too hard and possibly hurt your Horse physically. Your goal in becoming the Alpha is to become a benevolent herd leader who is always loved and respected. Every correction is done firmly but with love and to never hurt your Horse.

Your primary goal always is your own safety. Secondary is your Horse's safety. The reason to put your safety first, is that you are the most likely one to suffer an injury. The third goal is to always communicate love and respect. The fourth goal is to be the Alpha dominant Herd Leader. If you have a middle of the pecking order gelding, he will want to have you as the Alpha. He wants to have you to give him directions that he will follow. You as the alpha leader is perfectly natural for your Horse to accept. Work to display and exhibit the following Leader traits.

- Confident: A calm demeanor, steady stance, decisive firmness, strong yet happy vocalizing depicts a confident alpha. Be confident in your commands and guidance while combining these other alpha traits and your Horse will crave your leadership.

- Firm: Your Horse is doing something you don't like so you tell him no and you don't let him get away with it. You don't tolerate bad behavior. When you give him commands, you speak in a tone that is firm and easy. Additionally, giving him commands, you make him mind and you refuse to allow him to ignore you. When you speak, you make him pay attention.

- Unwavering: You want to give your Horse your undivided attention while working with him. You also want to be very focused. These two traits combined will help you get into your Horse's mind and make it clear what you want from him. Give him your unwavering attention during training.

- Clear: You can't give your Horse mixed signals and expect him to understand. He will get confused and let you down. If you want your Horse to stand, don't beckon him to come to you. Be mindful of the signals you give him and tell him the one thing you want him to do. Give him very clear, specific signals.

- Consistent: You can't condone a behavior one day and then punish it the next and think your Horse will understand. You must practice consistency. When he works hard or follows a command well, you must reward him the same way.

- Intelligent: You are the leader, which means you must be wise and show some wisdom and leadership. You must make intelligent decisions and show that you are smarter than your Horse. This is the only way to lead the way and be alpha. So even if your Horse tries to outsmart you, don't let him. Always have the dominant lead.

- Fearless: You should never hang back or be doubtful. Instead, you should want to take the lead without doubt, hesitation, or fear. You should be the one to lead when leading your Horse and you should not let him shove you out of the way when you let him outside, no matter how big he is. You cannot let him kick you or bite you. If he does something bad, you should discipline him. Tell him what to do without any fear and make him do it.

- Dominant: The more dominant you are, the more alpha you are. With your Horse, you want to be Herd Leader all the time. How does this look? It looks like you are not afraid to tell your Horse no, and when you tell him no he listens. You perform dominance training and train him without feeling bad or letting him walk all over you. You have rules in the stables that he must obey, and he does obey them because you have dominance over him. When you lead him, he walks proudly along at your heel and you reign him in when he tries to bound forward. Adopt these traits and you can become the alpha person that your Horse looks up to. Becoming alpha is something that starts right after the ride to the stables. You need to begin asserting your authority from day one. If you have an older horse, say a rescue, you can still begin the process. Even older horses can easily understand these kinds of communications. An older horse has likely learned everything else during his life.

Reminders for riding your Horse with a saddle

Find out from the previous owner what kind of bridle, reins, bit, and saddle were used on your Horse in the past. You should consider using the same type of equipment he was used to in the past. If you want to change some of his equipment, it is recommended that you do so gradually. Ask if your Horse has any quirks you should be aware of in advance of riding. Ride your Horse while you are meeting him the first time at his previous stables. Be sure that he seems like a good fit. Ask for a trial period. When you ride him test his leg cues, squeeze to make him walk, press in with left leg to turn right, and right leg to turn left, and then sit back in his saddle to ask him to stop. Test him with his reins, pull to the left to turn left and right to right, and pull back slightly to stop. Pull back further on the reins and squeeze his ribs slightly to see if he will back up a few steps.

If you are satisfied with the Horse's performance, then ask if you can do a trial period with the Horse. We will wish you well on building your new relationship with your Horse!

In Closing, I want to congratulate you on caring enough to learn how to adjust your behavior to improve your relationship with your Horse. Things will be better now, and you can curb problem behaviors since your Horse is under your alpha leadership.

Thank You!

Thank you *for taking the time to read this guide, and to train your Horse.*

Because . . .

You Absolutely Rock!

(Just ask your Horse :)

Legal Disclaimer:

The company publisher and its owners, officers, employees, contractors, and all participating or non-participant affiliates, along with the authors who have created this Saddle Up Horse Training How To Book and Guide and its content resources, titled Saddle Up Horse Training, by 'Horace Traynor' and published by Craicom, is held harmless against any and all claims and allegations against it. Further the aforementioned parties will ever be in any conceivable strategy, effort, direct or creatively obscure way responsible at any time for the action of your pet, not now or in the future. Animals, without warning, may cause injury to humans and or other animals. Horace Traynor, Craicom and all mentioned for the production and participation in creating the Saddle Up Horse Training Books, guides, Information, along with any and all outbound linked from or to resources are not in any way held accountable, or responsible for attacks, kicks, bites, mauling, or any other viciousness and or all other damages. We strongly recommend that you exercise caution for the safety of self, the animal, and around the animals while working with your horse. The company- publisher and its owners, officers, employees, contractors, and all participating or non-participant affiliates, along with the authors are not liable for any animal or human medical conditions or results obtained from training. While all attempts have been made to verify information provided in this publication, the company- publisher and its owners, officers, employees, contractors, and all participating or non-participant affiliates, along with the authors assume any responsibility for errors, omissions or contrary interpretation of the subject matter contained herein. The company publisher, authors and its owners, officers, employees, contractors, and all participating or non-participant affiliates, along with the authors assume no responsibility or liability whatsoever on the behalf of any purchaser or reader of the material provided. The owner of said horse training guide assumes any, and all risks associated with the methodology described inside the horse-training guidebook.

'Cedar'

Thanks for the Lessons Cedar.

Made in the USA
Las Vegas, NV
27 July 2023

75322000R00066